MAD LIBS®

HOT OFF THE PRESSES
MAD LIBS

concept created by Roger Price & Leonard Stern

PSS!
PRICE STERN SLOAN
An Imprint of Penguin Group (USA) Inc.

PRICE STERN SLOAN
Published by the Penguin Group
Penguin Group (USA) Inc., 375 Hudson Street, New York, New York 10014, USA
Penguin Group (Canada), 90 Eglinton Avenue East, Suite 700,
Toronto, Ontario M4P 2Y3, Canada
(a division of Pearson Penguin Canada Inc.)
Penguin Books Ltd., 80 Strand, London WC2R 0RL, England
Penguin Group Ireland, 25 St. Stephen's Green, Dublin 2, Ireland
(a division of Penguin Books Ltd.)
Penguin Group (Australia), 250 Camberwell Road, Camberwell, Victoria 3124, Australia
(a division of Pearson Australia Group Pty. Ltd.)
Penguin Books India Pvt. Ltd., 11 Community Centre,
Panchsheel Park, New Delhi—110 017, India
Penguin Group (NZ), 67 Apollo Drive, Rosedale, Auckland 0632, New Zealand
(a division of Pearson New Zealand Ltd.)
Penguin Books (South Africa) (Pty.) Ltd., 24 Sturdee Avenue,
Rosebank, Johannesburg 2196, South Africa

Penguin Books Ltd., Registered Offices:
80 Strand, London WC2R 0RL, England

Published by Price Stern Sloan,
a division of Penguin Young Readers Group,
345 Hudson Street, New York, New York 10014.

ISBN 978-0-8431-6999-7

3 5 7 9 10 8 6 4 2

MAD LIBS
INSTRUCTIONS

MAD LIBS® is a game for people who don't like games!
It can be played by one, two, three, four, or forty.

• RIDICULOUSLY SIMPLE DIRECTIONS

In this tablet you will find stories containing blank spaces where words are left out. One player, the READER, selects one of these stories. The READER does not tell anyone what the story is about. Instead, he/she asks the other players, the WRITERS, to give him/her words. These words are used to fill in the blank spaces in the story.

• TO PLAY

The READER asks each WRITER in turn to call out a word—an adjective or a noun or whatever the space calls for—and uses them to fill in the blank spaces in the story. The result is a MAD LIBS® game.

When the READER then reads the completed MAD LIBS® game to the other players, they will discover that they have written a story that is fantastic, screamingly funny, shocking, silly, crazy, or just plain dumb—depending upon which words each WRITER called out.

• EXAMPLE (*Before* and *After*)

" _____!" he said _____
　　　EXCLAMATION　　　　　　　　　　　ADVERB

as he jumped into his convertible _____ and
　　　　　　　　　　　　　　　　　　　NOUN

drove off with his _____ wife.
　　　　　　　　　ADJECTIVE

" __Ouch__!" he said __stupidly__
　　EXCLAMATION　　　　　　　ADVERB

as he jumped into his convertible __cat__ and
　　　　　　　　　　　　　　　　NOUN

drove off with his __brave__ wife.
　　　　　　　　ADJECTIVE

MAD LIBS
QUICK REVIEW

In case you have forgotten what adjectives, adverbs, nouns, and verbs are, here is a quick review:

An ADJECTIVE describes something or somebody. *Lumpy*, *soft*, *ugly*, *messy*, and *short* are adjectives.

An ADVERB tells how something is done. It modifies a verb and usually ends in "ly." *Modestly*, *stupidly*, *greedily*, and *carefully* are adverbs.

A NOUN is the name of a person, place, or thing. *Sidewalk*, *umbrella*, *bridle*, *bathtub*, and *nose* are nouns.

A VERB is an action word. *Run*, *pitch*, *jump*, and *swim* are verbs. Put the verbs in past tense if the directions say PAST TENSE. *Ran*, *pitched*, *jumped*, and *swam* are verbs in the past tense.

When we ask for A PLACE, we mean any sort of place: a country or city (*Spain*, *Cleveland*) or a room (*bathroom*, *kitchen*).

An EXCLAMATION or SILLY WORD is any sort of funny sound, gasp, grunt, or outcry, like *Wow!*, *Ouch!*, *Whomp!*, *Ick!*, and *Gadzooks!*

When we ask for specific words, like a NUMBER, a COLOR, an ANIMAL, or a PART OF THE BODY, we mean a word that is one of those things, like *seven*, *blue*, *horse*, or *head*.

When we ask for a PLURAL, it means more than one. For example, *cat* pluralized is *cats*.

MAD LIBS® is fun to play with friends, but you can also play it by yourself! To begin with, DO NOT look at the story on the page below. Fill in the blanks on this page with the words called for. Then, using the words you have selected, fill in the blank spaces in the story.

Now you've created your own hilarious MAD LIBS® game!

BEHIND THE SCENES

ADJECTIVE _____

ADJECTIVE _____

VERB ENDING IN "ING" _____

A PLACE _____

ADJECTIVE _____

PLURAL NOUN _____

PLURAL NOUN _____

VERB _____

ADJECTIVE _____

PART OF THE BODY (PLURAL) _____

VERB _____

PART OF THE BODY _____

SILLY WORD _____

ADJECTIVE _____

PLURAL NOUN _____

MAD LIBS

BEHIND THE SCENES

Putting on a newscast might look easy, but it takes a lot of

_____ work. Go behind the scenes, and you'll see dozens
 ADJECTIVE

of _____ workers _____ in every direction!
       ADJECTIVE   VERB ENDING IN "ING"

Reporters run back and forth between the studio and locations all

around (the) _____ to cover _____
                A PLACE   ADJECTIVE

stories and interview _____. They are joined by
                           PLURAL NOUN

videographers who operate handheld _____ to capture
                                          PLURAL NOUN

all the action. The anchors are the people who _____
                                                     VERB

behind the news desk and read the stories during the newscast. They

have to look _____ on air, so they can often be found
                ADJECTIVE

getting makeup applied to their _____. The
                                  PART OF THE BODY (PLURAL)

director tells everyone where and when to _____.
                                               VERB

It's easy to spot a director because he wears a headset on his

_____ and yells things like "Camera two!" and
   PART OF THE BODY

"Cut to commercial!" and "_____!" A newscast is
                              SILLY WORD

live television, so if you make a/an _____ mistake,
                                          ADJECTIVE

everyone watching at home on their _____ will know!
                                        PLURAL NOUN

MAD LIBS® is fun to play with friends, but you can also play it by yourself! To begin with, DO NOT look at the story on the page below. Fill in the blanks on this page with the words called for. Then, using the words you have selected, fill in the blank spaces in the story.

Now you've created your own hilarious MAD LIBS® game!

TODAY'S TOP STORIES

ADJECTIVE _____

NOUN _____

A PLACE _____

ADJECTIVE _____

PLURAL NOUN _____

NOUN _____

PERSON IN ROOM _____

NUMBER _____

PLURAL NOUN _____

PERSON IN ROOM _____

NOUN _____

PLURAL NOUN _____

ADJECTIVE _____

PLURAL NOUN _____

VERB ENDING IN "ING" _____

PLURAL NOUN _____

CELEBRITY (MALE) _____

PERSON IN ROOM (FEMALE) _____

ADJECTIVE _____

A PLACE _____

MAD LIBS
TODAY'S TOP STORIES

Good morning! Here are the _____ stories we're
<u>ADJECTIVE</u>

following today:

• A thirty-foot high _____ struck the coast of (the)
<u>NOUN</u>

_____ earlier today, causing _____
<u>A PLACE</u>   <u>ADJECTIVE</u>

flooding and forcing residents to flee to higher _____.
<u>PLURAL NOUN</u>

• A rare watercolor _____ by renowned fifteenth-century
<u>NOUN</u>

artist _____ Van Gogo sold at auction today for the
<u>PERSON IN ROOM</u>

record sum of _____ _____.
<u>NUMBER</u>   <u>PLURAL NOUN</u>

• _____ turns 113 today and is declared the oldest
<u>PERSON IN ROOM</u>

living _____ by the *Book of World* _____.
<u>NOUN</u>   <u>PLURAL NOUN</u>

• New, _____ research out of the University of _____
<u>ADJECTIVE</u>   <u>PLURAL NOUN</u>

concludes that thirty minutes of vigorous _____ can
<u>VERB ENDING IN "ING"</u>

help you lose up to ten _____ in a month.
<u>PLURAL NOUN</u>

• Hollywood heartthrob _____ has married longtime love
<u>CELEBRITY (MALE)</u>

_____ in a lavish, _____ ceremony in
<u>PERSON IN ROOM (FEMALE)</u>   <u>ADJECTIVE</u>

(the) _____.
<u>A PLACE</u>

MAD LIBS® is fun to play with friends, but you can also play it by yourself! To begin with, DO NOT look at the story on the page below. Fill in the blanks on this page with the words called for. Then, using the words you have selected, fill in the blank spaces in the story.

Now you've created your own hilarious MAD LIBS® game!

A MORNING PERSON

ADJECTIVE _____

NOUN _____

A PLACE _____

VERB ENDING IN "ING" _____

ANIMAL (PLURAL) _____

ADJECTIVE _____

NOUN _____

PERSON IN ROOM _____

ADJECTIVE _____

VERB ENDING IN "ING" _____

CELEBRITY _____

PERSON IN ROOM _____

NOUN _____

NUMBER _____

PLURAL NOUN _____

VERB _____

MAD LIBS

A MORNING PERSON

Are you cheery and _____ at the crack of dawn? Do you
                       ADJECTIVE

leap out of bed early in the morning, ready to greet the world with

a dazzling _____? As a journalist, can you quickly switch
              NOUN

gears from interviewing the ruler of (the) _____ to quizzing
                                              A PLACE

an expert on the effects of global _____ on the planet to
                                     VERB ENDING IN "ING"

judging a beauty contest for _____? Then *you* could
                                ANIMAL (PLURAL)

be the _____ morning show host we're looking for! The
          ADJECTIVE

number one–ranked show *Good Morning,* _____ is
                                           NOUN

searching for a cohost to join the current host, _____.
                                                   PERSON IN ROOM

The show combines _____, hard news stories with lighter
                     ADJECTIVE

pieces such as cooking and _____ segments, interviews
                              VERB ENDING IN "ING"

with A-listers like _____ and _____, and
                       CELEBRITY   PERSON IN ROOM

fashion tips such as one hundred stylish ways to wear a feathered

_____. Salary is $_____ a year plus a
   NOUN   NUMBER

generous allowance for clothing and _____. Are you
                                        PLURAL NOUN

qualified? Then _____ today for an application!
                   VERB

From HOT OFF THE PRESSES MAD LIBS® • Copyright © 2012 by Price Stern Sloan,
an imprint of Penguin Group (USA) Inc., 345 Hudson Street, New York, NY 10014.

MAD LIBS® is fun to play with friends, but you can also play it by yourself! To begin with, DO NOT look at the story on the page below. Fill in the blanks on this page with the words called for. Then, using the words you have selected, fill in the blank spaces in the story.

Now you've created your own hilarious MAD LIBS® game!

BREAKING NEWS: ALIEN ABDUCTION

NOUN _____

ADJECTIVE _____

A PLACE _____

ADJECTIVE _____

PERSON IN ROOM (FEMALE) _____

NOUN _____

ADJECTIVE _____

NOUN _____

TYPE OF LIQUID _____

PLURAL NOUN _____

PLURAL NOUN _____

PART OF THE BODY (PLURAL) _____

VERB (PAST TENSE) _____

COLOR _____

PART OF THE BODY (PLURAL) _____

NOUN _____

NOUN _____

ADJECTIVE _____

PART OF THE BODY (PLURAL) _____

MAD LIBS
BREAKING NEWS:
ALIEN ABDUCTION

The sighting of an unidentified flying _____ was
                                            NOUN
confirmed yesterday morning over the _____ skies of
                                            ADJECTIVE
(the) _____. Later that evening, a/an _____
         A PLACE   ADJECTIVE
resident named _____ told police she had been the
                  PERSON IN ROOM (FEMALE)
victim of a/an _____ abduction! "_____
                   NOUN   ADJECTIVE
creatures strapped me to a long _____ and made me
                                        NOUN
drink something that looked like _____ but tasted
                                      TYPE OF LIQUID
like rotten _____," she revealed. "Then they taped
               PLURAL NOUN
_____ all over my _____, and their
   PLURAL NOUN   PART OF THE BODY (PLURAL)
machines monitored me while I _____ nonstop
                                  VERB (PAST TENSE)
for what seemed like hours!" She described the aliens as having

large, _____ _____ and moving very
           COLOR   PART OF THE BODY (PLURAL)
gracefully—almost like a winged _____ in flight. "Finally
                                      NOUN
they placed me in a/an _____-shaped spacecraft and
                           NOUN
dropped me off in a/an _____ field," she said. "I wasn't
                           ADJECTIVE
hurt, but I learned that I prefer my _____ planted
                                        PART OF THE BODY (PLURAL)
firmly on the ground!"

From HOT OFF THE PRESSES MAD LIBS® • Copyright © 2012 by Price Stern Sloan,
an imprint of Penguin Group (USA) Inc., 345 Hudson Street, New York, NY 10014.

MAD LIBS® is fun to play with friends, but you can also play it by yourself! To begin with, DO NOT look at the story on the page below. Fill in the blanks on this page with the words called for. Then, using the words you have selected, fill in the blank spaces in the story.

Now you've created your own hilarious MAD LIBS® game!

ALL-ACCESS PRESS PASS

PERSON IN ROOM (FEMALE) _____

NOUN _____

NOUN _____

ADJECTIVE _____

COLOR _____

CELEBRITY (MALE) _____

PART OF THE BODY (PLURAL) _____

PERSON IN ROOM _____

ADJECTIVE _____

VERB (PAST TENSE) _____

ADJECTIVE _____

PLURAL NOUN _____

PLURAL NOUN _____

ADJECTIVE _____

PART OF THE BODY (PLURAL) _____

MAD☺LIBS®

ALL-ACCESS PRESS PASS

Hey there! _____ here, from WFUN-TV! Guess
PERSON IN ROOM (FEMALE)

what? I was the lucky _____ assigned to cover the annual
NOUN

_____ Awards and blog about it for you! So here are
NOUN

the _____ details! First, I hit the _____
ADJECTIVE COLOR

carpet and snagged interviews with everyone from the delicious

_____, who made me weak in the _____,
CELEBRITY (MALE) PART OF THE BODY (PLURAL)

to the current Hollywood "It" kid, _____, who's
PERSON IN ROOM

every bit as _____ in person as in the movies! I
ADJECTIVE

_____ backstage for most of the show because that's
VERB (PAST TENSE)

where all the _____ action was. And the after parties
ADJECTIVE

were amazing! People were toasting one another with glasses of

chilled _____. Finally everyone jumped into their
PLURAL NOUN

chauffeured _____ and sped home—everyone except
PLURAL NOUN

me, that is. Sadly, I had to use the only mode of transportation

available to a/an _____ reporter—my own two
ADJECTIVE

_____!
PART OF THE BODY (PLURAL)

MAD LIBS® is fun to play with friends, but you can also play it by yourself! To begin with, DO NOT look at the story on the page below. Fill in the blanks on this page with the words called for. Then, using the words you have selected, fill in the blank spaces in the story.

Now you've created your own hilarious MAD LIBS® game!

SPORTS RECAP

NOUN _____

SILLY WORD _____

PART OF THE BODY _____

ADJECTIVE _____

NOUN _____

PLURAL NOUN _____

ADJECTIVE _____

PART OF THE BODY (PLURAL) _____

VERB _____

SAME VERB _____

PLURAL NOUN _____

PERSON IN ROOM _____

NOUN _____

ADJECTIVE _____

VERB ENDING IN "ING" _____

NOUN _____

PART OF THE BODY _____

NOUN _____

ADJECTIVE _____

ADJECTIVE _____

It was the final game of the National _____-ball
NOUN

Championships, and—_____!—it was a/an _____-
SILLY WORD PART OF THE BODY

biter! The hometown team, the _____ Mudslingers,
ADJECTIVE

was losing by just one _____. The _____
NOUN PLURAL NOUN

were loaded, but the team was down to its last _____
ADJECTIVE

batter—and the final pitch. The sold-out crowd was on its

_____, screaming "_____, Mudslingers,
PART OF THE BODY (PLURAL) VERB

_____!" and waving giant foam _____.
SAME VERB PLURAL NOUN

The pitch to star player _____ was perfect, and—
PERSON IN ROOM

crack!—the _____ was airborne. The _____
NOUN ADJECTIVE

outfielder took off _____ toward the fence with his
VERB ENDING IN "ING"

_____ outstretched to catch the ball—but all he could
NOUN

do was watch it sail over his _____ and into the stands.
PART OF THE BODY

One _____ scored, then another! The crowd went
NOUN

absolutely _____! The Mudslingers won the game that
ADJECTIVE

day—and the hearts of their _____ fans forever!
ADJECTIVE

From HOT OFF THE PRESSES MAD LIBS® • Copyright © 2012 by Price Stern Sloan,
an imprint of Penguin Group (USA) Inc., 345 Hudson Street, New York, NY 10014.

MAD LIBS® is fun to play with friends, but you can also play it by yourself! To begin with, DO NOT look at the story on the page below. Fill in the blanks on this page with the words called for. Then, using the words you have selected, fill in the blank spaces in the story.

Now you've created your own hilarious MAD LIBS® game!

MAN ON THE STREET INTERVIEWS

A PLACE _____

ADJECTIVE _____

PERSON IN ROOM (FEMALE) _____

A PLACE _____

PLURAL NOUN _____

NOUN _____

NOUN _____

CELEBRITY _____

NOUN _____

PART OF THE BODY (PLURAL) _____

ADJECTIVE _____

PERSON IN ROOM _____

A PLACE _____

PART OF THE BODY _____

VERB _____

PERSON IN ROOM (MALE) _____

NOUN _____

MAD LIBS®
MAN ON THE STREET INTERVIEWS

This is roving reporter Perry Winkle, and I'm here in (the)

_____ to ask folks today's random question: *What is the*
<u>A PLACE</u>

first thing you would do if you ruled the world? Responses ranged from

intelligent to downright _____. Here's a sampling:
<u>ADJECTIVE</u>

- _____ from (the) _____ said, "I'd
  <u>PERSON IN ROOM (FEMALE)</u>   <u>A PLACE</u>

  make sure everyone had plenty of healthy _____ to
  <u>PLURAL NOUN</u>

  eat and a warm, safe _____ to live in."
  <u>NOUN</u>

- An up-and-coming _____ by the name of _____
  <u>NOUN</u>   <u>CELEBRITY</u>

  said, "I would give each man, woman, and _____ a job.
  <u>NOUN</u>

  It's important to use your mind or your _____ to
  <u>PART OF THE BODY (PLURAL)</u>

  work and make the world a/an _____ place."
  <u>ADJECTIVE</u>

- _____ from (the) _____ said, "There'd be no
  <u>PERSON IN ROOM</u>   <u>A PLACE</u>

  wars. People would only be allowed to _____ wrestle one
  <u>PART OF THE BODY</u>

  another, but then they'd _____ and make up."
  <u>VERB</u>

- Local comedian _____ said, "I would require every
  <u>PERSON IN ROOM (MALE)</u>

  citizen to address me by my superhero name—_____-man!"
  <u>NOUN</u>

MAD LIBS® is fun to play with friends, but you can also play it by yourself! To begin with, DO NOT look at the story on the page below. Fill in the blanks on this page with the words called for. Then, using the words you have selected, fill in the blank spaces in the story.

Now you've created your own hilarious MAD LIBS® game!

TRAFFIC REPORT

PLURAL NOUN _____

ADJECTIVE _____

VERB _____

NUMBER _____

NOUN _____

A PLACE _____

PLURAL NOUN _____

ADJECTIVE _____

PART OF THE BODY (PLURAL) _____

NOUN _____

CELEBRITY _____

ADJECTIVE _____

PLURAL NOUN _____

NOUN _____

PERSON IN ROOM _____

NOUN _____

NOUN _____

NOUN _____

MAD LIBS

TRAFFIC REPORT

Folks, I hate to be the bearer of bad _____, but it's a slow-

                      PLURAL NOUN

go on today's _____ roadways. Everyone seems to have

          ADJECTIVE

forgotten how to _____ behind the wheel! There's a/an

              VERB

_____-_____ pileup on Route 86 that's got traffic

  NUMBER   NOUN

backed up all the way to (the) _____! Police and emergency

                  A PLACE

_____ are on the scene, but those _____

PLURAL NOUN   ADJECTIVE

drivers craning their _____ to see what's going on

                PART OF THE BODY (PLURAL)

aren't helping matters. A car with a flat _____ is causing

                        NOUN

a slowdown on _____ Highway. A/An _____

          CELEBRITY   ADJECTIVE

semitruck headed downtown has jackknifed, spilling its load of

frozen _____. And here's something you don't see every

     PLURAL NOUN

day: a two-hundred-pound _____ by the name of

                    NOUN

_____ escaped from the zoo and wandered into the path

PERSON IN ROOM

of an oncoming _____, which then swerved and crashed

              NOUN

into a/an _____. Let's face it, folks—today's a day where

       NOUN

you need patience, a sense of humor, or a flying _____!

                                NOUN

From HOT OFF THE PRESSES MAD LIBS® • Copyright © 2012 by Price Stern Sloan,
an imprint of Penguin Group (USA) Inc., 345 Hudson Street, New York, NY 10014.

MAD LIBS® is fun to play with friends, but you can also play it by yourself! To begin with, DO NOT look at the story on the page below. Fill in the blanks on this page with the words called for. Then, using the words you have selected, fill in the blank spaces in the story.

Now you've created your own hilarious MAD LIBS® game!

THAT'S CLASSIFIED INFORMATION

ADJECTIVE _____

ADJECTIVE _____

NOUN _____

PERSON IN ROOM _____

ADJECTIVE _____

PLURAL NOUN _____

NUMBER _____

PLURAL NOUN _____

PLURAL NOUN _____

NOUN _____

NOUN _____

ADJECTIVE _____

PLURAL NOUN _____

NOUN _____

PLURAL NOUN _____

ADJECTIVE _____

PLURAL NOUN _____

MAD LIBS®
THAT'S CLASSIFIED INFORMATION

Got junk? Sell your unwanted stuff in our _____
ADJECTIVE

classified section! Today's _____ deals include a/an:
ADJECTIVE

• baby grand _____ previously owned by legendary
NOUN

pianist _____ "_____ Hands" O'Hara.
PERSON IN ROOM   ADJECTIVE

Asking two thousand _____ or best offer
PLURAL NOUN

• _____-piece collection of rare _____ finely crafted
NUMBER   PLURAL NOUN

from ceramic, porcelain, and gold-plated _____
PLURAL NOUN

• cage, feeding bowl, and hand-knitted _____ for a
NOUN

pet _____
NOUN

• _____ minifridge, perfect for holding bottles of
ADJECTIVE

_____
PLURAL NOUN

• used pickup _____ with one hundred thousand _____
NOUN   PLURAL NOUN

and _____ bumper sticker stating "Honk if you love
ADJECTIVE

_____!"
PLURAL NOUN

MAD LIBS® is fun to play with friends, but you can also play it by yourself! To begin with, DO NOT look at the story on the page below. Fill in the blanks on this page with the words called for. Then, using the words you have selected, fill in the blank spaces in the story.

Now you've created your own hilarious MAD LIBS® game!

TALK SHOW QUEEN

NUMBER _____

NOUN _____

PERSON IN ROOM (FEMALE) _____

ADJECTIVE _____

PART OF THE BODY _____

NOUN _____

PERSON IN ROOM (MALE) _____

CELEBRITY (FEMALE) _____

PART OF THE BODY _____

NUMBER _____

NOUN _____

NOUN _____

ADJECTIVE _____

ADJECTIVE _____

A PLACE _____

MAD LIBS®
TALK SHOW QUEEN

After a/an _____-year reign as daytime TV's most
　　　　　　　　　NUMBER

popular talk show _____, _____
　　　　　　　　　　NOUN　　　　　　　PERSON IN ROOM (FEMALE)

O'Walters finally announced her retirement. On her _____
　　　　　　　　　　　　　　　　　　　　　　　　ADJECTIVE

farewell show, she recalled the moments nearest and dearest to her

_____ _____:
PART OF THE BODY

• When famed Hollywood actor and leading _____,
　　　　　　　　　　　　　　　　　　　　　　　　NOUN

_____, proclaimed his love for _____—
PERSON IN ROOM (MALE)　　　　　　　　　　　CELEBRITY (FEMALE)

then surprised everyone by getting down on one _____
　　　　　　　　　　　　　　　　　　　　　　　PART OF THE BODY

and proposing with a/an _____-karat diamond _____.
　　　　　　　　　　　　　NUMBER　　　　　　　　　　NOUN

• When a woman and the _____ she gave up for adoption
　　　　　　　　　　　　　NOUN

twenty years earlier were reunited.

• When each member of the ___ _____ audience was given
　　　　　　　　　　　　　　　ADJECTIVE

a fully loaded, fuel-efficient _____ convertible and an
　　　　　　　　　　　　　　　ADJECTIVE

all-expenses-paid trip to (the) _____.
　　　　　　　　　　　　　　　A PLACE

MAD LIBS® is fun to play with friends, but you can also play it by yourself! To begin with, DO NOT look at the story on the page below. Fill in the blanks on this page with the words called for. Then, using the words you have selected, fill in the blank spaces in the story.

Now you've created your own hilarious MAD LIBS® game!

BREAKING NEWS: BIGFOOT SPOTTED

NOUN _____

NOUN _____

ADJECTIVE _____

PART OF THE BODY _____

NOUN _____

PLURAL NOUN _____

PLURAL NOUN _____

PLURAL NOUN _____

PERSON IN ROOM _____

NOUN _____

ANIMAL _____

PART OF THE BODY (PLURAL) _____

VERB ENDING IN "ING" _____

VERB ENDING IN "ING" _____

PART OF THE BODY _____

PERSON IN ROOM _____

VERB (PAST TENSE) _____

BREAKING NEWS: BIGFOOT SPOTTED

A/An _____ Scout troop camping in a remote
_____NOUN_____

location inside _____ National Forest reported a/an
_____NOUN

_____ encounter with the elusive creature known as
ADJECTIVE

Big-_____. "It was dusk. The _____ had
____PART OF THE BODY_____NOUN

just begun to set when we finished pitching our _____.
_____PLURAL NOUN

We set out to gather _____ to make a fire so we
_____PLURAL NOUN

could roast some _____ for s'mores," said troop
_____PLURAL NOUN

leader _____. "We were just about to head back
____PERSON IN ROOM

to camp when we heard a/an _____ snap loudly
_____NOUN

nearby. We figured it was a squirrel or a/an _____,
_____ANIMAL

but then we saw a pair of _____ watching us
_____PART OF THE BODY (PLURAL)

from the darkness." The troop leader told how they took off

_____ as fast as they could through the forest and
VERB ENDING IN "ING"

hid inside their _____ bags all night. "I was scared out
_____VERB ENDING IN "ING"

of my _____," said nine-year-old _____.
____PART OF THE BODY_____PERSON IN ROOM

"I don't think I _____ more than five minutes all
_____VERB (PAST TENSE)

night."

MAD LIBS® is fun to play with friends, but you can also play it by yourself! To begin with, DO NOT look at the story on the page below. Fill in the blanks on this page with the words called for. Then, using the words you have selected, fill in the blank spaces in the story.

Now you've created your own hilarious MAD LIBS® game!

CONCERT REVIEW

ADJECTIVE _____

COLOR _____

ANIMAL (PLURAL) _____

VERB ENDING IN "ING" _____

PLURAL NOUN _____

PERSON IN ROOM _____

PART OF THE BODY _____

PART OF THE BODY (PLURAL) _____

ADJECTIVE _____

PLURAL NOUN _____

ADJECTIVE _____

NOUN _____

VERB ENDING IN "ING" _____

ADJECTIVE _____

PERSON IN ROOM (FEMALE) _____

PART OF THE BODY _____

COLOR _____

ARTICLE OF CLOTHING _____

NOUN _____

PLURAL NOUN _____

MAD LIBS®
CONCERT REVIEW

The _____ _____ _____
      ADJECTIVE   COLOR   ANIMAL (PLURAL)

performed last night and wowed the _____-room-only
                                   VERB ENDING IN "ING"

crowd of screaming _____. Music Editor _____
                      PLURAL NOUN   PERSON IN ROOM

was there and had this to report:

"What a/an _____-blowing show! My _____
         PART OF THE BODY   PART OF THE BODY (PLURAL)

are still ringing! The band performed all their _____ hits,
                                    ADJECTIVE

like "Too Cool for _____" and "Best _____ Friends
                PLURAL NOUN   ADJECTIVE

Forever." Between the music and the awesome laser _____
                                           NOUN

show, the crowd was on its feet and _____ to the beat
                               VERB ENDING IN "ING"

the whole night. But the music and lights were almost overshadowed

by the many _____ costume changes by lead singer
                  ADJECTIVE

Lady _____. It was hard to decide which was
          PERSON IN ROOM (FEMALE)

more _____-dropping—the _____ leather
       PART OF THE BODY   COLOR

_____ and _____-shaped headpiece she wore
  ARTICLE OF CLOTHING   NOUN

or the simple gown fashioned completely from _____."
                                          PLURAL NOUN

From HOT OFF THE PRESSES MAD LIBS® • Copyright © 2012 by Price Stern Sloan,
an imprint of Penguin Group (USA) Inc., 345 Hudson Street, New York, NY 10014.

MAD LIBS® is fun to play with friends, but you can also play it by yourself! To begin with, DO NOT look at the story on the page below. Fill in the blanks on this page with the words called for. Then, using the words you have selected, fill in the blank spaces in the story.

Now you've created your own hilarious MAD LIBS® game!

AND IN LOCAL NEWS

ADJECTIVE _____

NOUN _____

PLURAL NOUN _____

NOUN _____

NOUN _____

PERSON IN ROOM _____

NOUN _____

NOUN _____

NOUN _____

ADJECTIVE _____

NOUN _____

PLURAL NOUN _____

PLURAL NOUN _____

ADJECTIVE _____

PLURAL NOUN _____

NOUN _____

MAD LIBS
AND IN LOCAL NEWS

Small town life doesn't mean big things don't happen! Here are some

of the _____ events taking place this weekend and next
             ADJECTIVE

in Little _____ Falls:
                NOUN

• Stop by the Brotherhood of the _____ Lodge on Sunday
                                    PLURAL NOUN

 for an all-you-can-eat _____ breakfast to benefit the
                            NOUN

 town's _____ rescue shelter. Mayor _____ will
           NOUN   PERSON IN ROOM

 be flipping hotcakes and grilling _____ patties.
                                        NOUN

• Join us for the grand opening of the town's first _____
                                                        NOUN

 Mart! A limited edition _____ will be given away to
                            NOUN

 the first one hundred _____ shoppers.
                          ADJECTIVE

• Next weekend is the annual _____ festival. Vendors will be
                                NOUN

 selling fresh-picked _____, and baked _____ will
                        PLURAL NOUN   PLURAL NOUN

 be available. Come hungry—and leave _____!
                                        ADJECTIVE

• Mark your calendar for the community garage sale. Unearth your

 unused _____ and sell them for a few bucks. Remember—
           PLURAL NOUN

 one man's _____ is another man's treasure!
                NOUN

From HOT OFF THE PRESSES MAD LIBS® • Copyright © 2012 by Price Stern Sloan,
an imprint of Penguin Group (USA) Inc., 345 Hudson Street, New York, NY 10014.

MAD LIBS® is fun to play with friends, but you can also play it by yourself! To begin with, DO NOT look at the story on the page below. Fill in the blanks on this page with the words called for. Then, using the words you have selected, fill in the blank spaces in the story.

Now you've created your own hilarious MAD LIBS® game!

WARNING: SEVERE WEATHER

ADJECTIVE _____

A PLACE _____

ADJECTIVE _____

PLURAL NOUN _____

PLURAL NOUN _____

VERB ENDING IN "ING" _____

NOUN _____

ADJECTIVE _____

NOUN _____

NOUN _____

PART OF THE BODY _____

NOUN _____

VERB ENDING IN "ING" _____

TYPE OF LIQUID _____

VERB _____

PART OF THE BODY (PLURAL) _____

ADJECTIVE _____

Our radar shows a line of _____ weather stretching from
ADJECTIVE

the midwest plains all the way to the coast of (the) _____.
A PLACE

This weather pattern is producing _____ thunderstorms
ADJECTIVE

with heavy rains, _____ gusting up to eighty mph,
PLURAL NOUN

and hail the size of _____! Tornado warnings are
PLURAL NOUN

in effect for most of the viewing area. A funnel cloud was spotted

_____ across an open field and destroying every
VERB ENDING IN "ING"

_____ in its path. Remember, in the event of a/an
NOUN

_____ tornado, head to the basement or climb into
ADJECTIVE

the nearest _____ and pull a/an _____
NOUN   NOUN

over you so that your _____ is protected. If you're
PART OF THE BODY

out driving around in your _____, be on the lookout
NOUN

for flash _____ in low-lying areas. If you get caught
VERB ENDING IN "ING"

in rushing _____, climb out of your vehicle and
TYPE OF LIQUID

_____ for your life! Stay tuned to this channel—and
VERB

keep your _____ to the sky—for _____
PART OF THE BODY (PLURAL)   ADJECTIVE

weather-related updates.

MAD LIBS® is fun to play with friends, but you can also play it by yourself! To begin with, DO NOT look at the story on the page below. Fill in the blanks on this page with the words called for. Then, using the words you have selected, fill in the blank spaces in the story.

Now you've created your own hilarious MAD LIBS® game!

HOW TO GET THE SCOOP

ADJECTIVE _____

ADJECTIVE _____

NOUN _____

VERB _____

NOUN _____

NOUN _____

PART OF THE BODY _____

ADJECTIVE _____

VERB ENDING IN "ING" _____

PLURAL NOUN _____

PLURAL NOUN _____

ADJECTIVE _____

NOUN _____

PLURAL NOUN _____

VERB ENDING IN "ING" _____

ADJECTIVE _____

MAD☺LIBS®
HOW TO GET THE SCOOP

Do you have a/an _____ nose for news? Here are
                        ADJECTIVE
_____ tips for becoming a/an _____-winning
   ADJECTIVE   NOUN
investigative journalist:

1. March up to a person's front door and _____. When they
                                              VERB
   answer the _____, stick your micro-_____
                  NOUN   NOUN
   right under their _____ and start firing questions.
                       PART OF THE BODY

2. Ask as many _____ questions as possible. Getting
                     ADJECTIVE
   someone to break down and start _____ is great.
                                     VERB ENDING IN "ING"

3. Seek out a person's family and _____. Offer them
                                     PLURAL NOUN
   large amounts of _____ to tell you everything they know.
                      PLURAL NOUN

4. Assemble a/an _____ disguise to go undercover. An
                    ADJECTIVE
   oversize _____ to wear across your face and a fake
               NOUN
   pair of _____ work well.
              PLURAL NOUN

5. Practice _____ as fast as you can so, when necessary,
               VERB ENDING IN "ING"
   you can make a/an _____ getaway.
                        ADJECTIVE

From HOT OFF THE PRESSES MAD LIBS® • Copyright © 2012 by Price Stern Sloan,
an imprint of Penguin Group (USA) Inc., 345 Hudson Street, New York, NY 10014.

MAD LIBS® is fun to play with friends, but you can also play it by yourself! To begin with, DO NOT look at the story on the page below. Fill in the blanks on this page with the words called for. Then, using the words you have selected, fill in the blank spaces in the story.

Now you've created your own hilarious MAD LIBS® game!

SUMMER MOVIE REVIEWS

ADJECTIVE _____

NOUN _____

NOUN _____

PLURAL NOUN _____

PERSON IN ROOM (MALE) _____

ADJECTIVE _____

ADJECTIVE _____

PLURAL NOUN _____

ADJECTIVE _____

PERSON IN ROOM (MALE) _____

ANIMAL _____

SAME ANIMAL _____

ADJECTIVE _____

VERB _____

PERSON IN ROOM (FEMALE) _____

NOUN _____

ADJECTIVE _____

PLURAL NOUN _____

PERSON IN ROOM (MALE) _____

MAD LIBS

SUMMER MOVIE REVIEWS

It's summer, and you know what that means: _____
ADJECTIVE

weather, icy-cold _____-sicles, and big blockbusters. Check
NOUN

out what's coming to a/an _____ near you this summer!
NOUN

• _____ of the Caribbean: Captain _____
PLURAL NOUN   PERSON IN ROOM (MALE)

and his band of _____ scalawags take to the _____
ADJECTIVE   ADJECTIVE

seas in search of buried _____.
PLURAL NOUN

• The Big _____ Ogre: A cranky ogre named
ADJECTIVE

_____, his sidekick—a/an _____
PERSON IN ROOM (MALE)   ANIMAL

named _____—and a/an _____ gang of
SAME ANIMAL   ADJECTIVE

fairy tale creatures go on a search and _____ mission to
VERB

rescue Princess _____ from a tower guarded by a fire-
PERSON IN ROOM (FEMALE)

breathing _____.
NOUN

• The Boy Wizard: A/An _____ boy discovers he
ADJECTIVE

possesses magical _____ that he must use to defeat the
PLURAL NOUN

evil wizard, Lord _____.
PERSON IN ROOM (MALE)

MAD LIBS® is fun to play with friends, but you can also play it by yourself! To begin with, DO NOT look at the story on the page below. Fill in the blanks on this page with the words called for. Then, using the words you have selected, fill in the blank spaces in the story.

Now you've created your own hilarious MAD LIBS® game!

CELEBRITY INTERVIEW

VERB _____

NOUN _____

PERSON IN ROOM _____

PART OF THE BODY _____

ADJECTIVE _____

NOUN _____

ADJECTIVE _____

NOUN _____

ADJECTIVE _____

ADJECTIVE _____

PLURAL NOUN _____

PART OF THE BODY _____

NOUN _____

ADJECTIVE _____

NUMBER _____

MAD LIBS
CELEBRITY INTERVIEW

Movie critic Daisy Meadows had the chance to _____
                                                        VERB
with international _____ star Brad Kluney and chat
                          NOUN
about his new project, *The* _____ *Chronicles*.
                                   PERSON IN ROOM
Daisy: Forgive me if I'm a bit _____-tied. I'm such a/an
                                          PART OF THE BODY
_____ fan of yours! You're the handsomest _____
      ADJECTIVE   NOUN
I've ever laid eyes on.

Brad: That's so _____ of you to say.
                          ADJECTIVE
Daisy: So, Brad, in this movie, are you a good _____ or
                                                              NOUN
a/an _____ guy?
           ADJECTIVE
Brad: I play a/an _____ guy who gets mixed up with some
                              ADJECTIVE
_____ who may or may not be on the wrong side of the law. I
   PLURAL NOUN
spend a lot of the movie thoughtfully scratching my _____.
                                                             PART OF THE BODY
Daisy: There's already buzz that this role will earn you a/an

_____ Award nomination.
      NOUN
Brad: A happy, _____ audience is all I want—and my
                          ADJECTIVE
_____ dollar salary.
      NUMBER

From HOT OFF THE PRESSES MAD LIBS® • Copyright © 2012 by Price Stern Sloan,
an imprint of Penguin Group (USA) Inc., 345 Hudson Street, New York, NY 10014.

MAD LIBS® is fun to play with friends, but you can also play it by yourself! To begin with, DO NOT look at the story on the page below. Fill in the blanks on this page with the words called for. Then, using the words you have selected, fill in the blank spaces in the story.

Now you've created your own hilarious MAD LIBS® game!

BREAKING NEWS: LOST CITY FOUND

ADJECTIVE _____

A PLACE _____

ADJECTIVE _____

SILLY WORD _____

PLURAL NOUN _____

ADJECTIVE _____

PLURAL NOUN _____

PART OF THE BODY _____

ANIMAL _____

PART OF THE BODY _____

ANIMAL _____

CELEBRITY _____

ADJECTIVE _____

NOUN _____

PERSON IN ROOM _____

PART OF THE BODY (PLURAL) _____

A/An _____ archeological team working in the remote
ADJECTIVE

jungles of (the) _____ have reportedly discovered the
A PLACE

_____ ancient city of _____ buried under about
ADJECTIVE   SILLY WORD

ten miles of _____. The team said they knew they had
PLURAL NOUN

stumbled onto something _____ when they unearthed
ADJECTIVE

weapons, tools, and _____ handcrafted from pure
PLURAL NOUN

gold and bearing the city's symbol—a mythical creature with the

_____ of a/an _____ and the _____
PART OF THE BODY   ANIMAL   PART OF THE BODY

of a/an _____. If that weren't proof enough, Chief
ANIMAL

Archeologist Dr. _____ said they were certain it was the
CELEBRITY

ancient city when they found a tomb marked with the name of the

city's legendary, _____ ruler, Ah-Ah-Achooey-Kaboom-
ADJECTIVE

Boom, which roughly translates to "one who sneezes as explosively as

a/an _____ erupting." "It's incredible," said Junior Archeologist
NOUN

_____. "I never would have believed this place existed if I
PERSON IN ROOM

hadn't seen it with my own two _____."
PART OF THE BODY (PLURAL)

MAD LIBS® is fun to play with friends, but you can also play it by yourself! To begin with, DO NOT look at the story on the page below. Fill in the blanks on this page with the words called for. Then, using the words you have selected, fill in the blank spaces in the story.

Now you've created your own hilarious MAD LIBS® game!

DARE TO BE NEWSWORTHY

PLURAL NOUN _____

ADJECTIVE _____

PERSON IN ROOM (MALE) _____

NOUN _____

PLURAL NOUN _____

ARTICLE OF CLOTHING _____

PERSON IN ROOM (FEMALE) _____

COLOR _____

VERB (PAST TENSE) _____

PLURAL NOUN _____

PERSON IN ROOM (MALE) _____

NUMBER _____

PLURAL NOUN _____

PART OF THE BODY _____

A PLACE _____

A PLACE _____

PERSON IN ROOM (FEMALE) _____

CELEBRITY (MALE) _____

MAD LIBS®
DARE TO BE NEWSWORTHY

Some people will do anything to get their fifteen minutes

of _____. Think you've seen it all? Check out the
       PLURAL NOUN

_____ things these people did to make headlines:
       ADJECTIVE

- _____, a star _____-ball player at his
  PERSON IN ROOM (MALE)   NOUN

  school, ran a marathon wearing 5-inch stiletto _____
                                                  PLURAL NOUN

  and a skintight, floral _____.
                          ARTICLE OF CLOTHING

- _____ painted herself bright _____
  PERSON IN ROOM (FEMALE)   COLOR

  and _____ in a public fountain while people blasted
      VERB (PAST TENSE)

  her with squirt guns filled with _____.
                                   PLURAL NOUN

- _____ tied _____ helium-filled
  PERSON IN ROOM (MALE)   NUMBER

  _____ around his _____ and floated
  PLURAL NOUN   PART OF THE BODY

  from (the) _____ to (the) _____.
             A PLACE   A PLACE

- _____ walked up to every fast-food drive-through
  PERSON IN ROOM (FEMALE)

  window in town and asked if she could have _____ to go.
                                             CELEBRITY (MALE)

MAD LIBS® is fun to play with friends, but you can also play it by yourself! To begin with, DO NOT look at the story on the page below. Fill in the blanks on this page with the words called for. Then, using the words you have selected, fill in the blank spaces in the story.

Now you've created your own hilarious MAD LIBS® game!

POLITICAL DEBATE

ADJECTIVE _____

COLOR _____

NOUN _____

ADJECTIVE _____

VERB ENDING IN "ING" _____

NOUN _____

PLURAL NOUN _____

ADJECTIVE _____

PLURAL NOUN _____

ADJECTIVE _____

NOUN _____

TYPE OF LIQUID _____

MAD LIBS®
POLITICAL DEBATE

Welcome to another edition of *Meet the* _____ *Candidates*!
                                          ADJECTIVE

Today we have Jessica and Justin from _____ Valley
                                          COLOR

High School. Both of them are running for student council

_____. Let's listen as they share their _____
    NOUN   ADJECTIVE

ideas for leadership.

Jessica: I believe that teachers should assign _____
                                                  VERB ENDING IN "ING"

homework every night.

Justin: I will fight for the cafeteria's right to serve _____ tots
                                                            NOUN

every day at lunch and steamed _____ only once a week.
                                PLURAL NOUN

Jessica: I will make sure our library is stocked with the latest

_____ best sellers.
    ADJECTIVE

Justin: I will keep our vending machines stocked with _____.
                                                          PLURAL NOUN

Jessica: A vote for me is a vote for a clean, safe, _____
                                                        ADJECTIVE

school where each and every _____ can excel!
                             NOUN

Justin: A vote for me ensures drinking fountains are filled with clean,

fresh _____. Yum!
      TYPE OF LIQUID

From HOT OFF THE PRESSES MAD LIBS® • Copyright © 2012 by Price Stern Sloan,
an imprint of Penguin Group (USA) Inc., 345 Hudson Street, New York, NY 10014.

MAD LIBS® is fun to play with friends, but you can also play it by yourself! To begin with, DO NOT look at the story on the page below. Fill in the blanks on this page with the words called for. Then, using the words you have selected, fill in the blank spaces in the story.

Now you've created your own hilarious MAD LIBS® game!

LOCAL HERO BECOMES SENSATION

PERSON IN ROOM (MALE) _____

ADJECTIVE _____

NOUN _____

A PLACE _____

VERB ENDING IN "ING" _____

NOUN _____

PLURAL NOUN _____

VERB _____

ADJECTIVE _____

PART OF THE BODY _____

NOUN _____

ADJECTIVE _____

NOUN _____

PART OF THE BODY _____

TYPE OF LIQUID _____

NOUN _____

PERSON IN ROOM (FEMALE) _____

PART OF THE BODY _____

NOUN _____

_____ "The Truck" MacAllister didn't consider himself
PERSON IN ROOM (MALE)

a hero—except when he made a/an _____ play on the
ADJECTIVE

_____-ball field. But residents of (the) _____
NOUN   A PLACE

begged to differ. MacAllister happened to be _____
                                              VERB ENDING IN "ING"

by a bank when a masked _____ came running out
                          NOUN

carrying a bag of stolen _____. MacAllister didn't stop
                          PLURAL NOUN

to _____—he just sprinted after the _____
    VERB   ADJECTIVE

thief and tackled him. MacAllister held the robber in a/an

_____-lock until police arrived. He didn't know
PART OF THE BODY

that a pedestrian had caught it all on video and posted it on

_____-Tube. It was a/an _____ hit, and
NOUN   ADJECTIVE

MacAllister became an overnight _____! Strangers
                                  NOUN

wanted to shake his _____. Restaurants gave him
                      PART OF THE BODY

free _____. A lovely _____ named
      TYPE OF LIQUID   NOUN

_____ even proposed marriage! But he never let
PERSON IN ROOM (FEMALE)

fame go to his _____. "I'm just a simple _____
                PART OF THE BODY   NOUN

who was in the right place at the right time," he said.

This book is published by

PSS!

PRICE STERN SLOAN

whose other splendid titles include
such literary classics as

Ad Lib Mad Libs®

Best of Mad Libs®

Camp Daze Mad Libs®

Christmas Carol Mad Libs®

Christmas Fun Mad Libs®

Cool Mad Libs®

Dance Mania Mad Libs®

Dear Valentine Letters Mad Libs®

Dinosaur Mad Libs®

Diva Girl Mad Libs®

Dude, Where's My Mad Libs®

Family Tree Mad Libs®

Fun in the Sun Mad Libs®

Girls Just Wanna Have Mad Libs®

Goofy Mad Libs®

Grab Bag Mad Libs®

Graduation Mad Libs®

Grand Slam Mad Libs®

Happily Ever Mad Libs®

Happy Birthday Mad Libs®

Haunted Mad Libs®

Holly, Jolly Mad Libs®

Kid Libs Mad Libs®

Letters from Camp Mad Libs®

Letters to Mom & Dad Mad Libs®

Mad About Animals Mad Libs®

Mad Libs® for President

Mad Libs® from Outer Space

Mad Libs® in Love

Mad Libs® on the Road

Mad Mad Mad Mad Mad Libs®

Monster Mad Libs®

More Best of Mad Libs®

Night of the Living Mad Libs®

Ninjas Mad Libs®

Off-the-Wall Mad Libs®

The Original #1 Mad Libs®

P. S. I Love Mad Libs®

Peace, Love, and Mad Libs®

Pirates Mad Libs®

Prime-Time Mad Libs®

Rock 'n' Roll Mad Libs®

Slam Dunk Mad Libs®

Sleepover Party Mad Libs®

Son of Mad Libs®

Sooper Dooper Mad Libs®

Spooky Mad Libs®

Straight "A" Mad Libs®

Totally Pink Mad Libs®

Undead Mad Libs®

Upside Down Mad Libs®

Vacation Fun Mad Libs®

We Wish You a Merry Mad Libs®

Winter Games Mad Libs®

You've Got Mad Libs®

and many, many more!
Mad Libs® are available wherever books are sold.